Cleopatra

The story of the beautiful Egyptian queen

Cleopatra

The story of the beautiful Egyptian queen

VALERIE WILDING

A & C Black • London

For my long-time friend, Julia Burns, with love

First published 2010 by
A & C Black Publishers Ltd
36 Soho Square, London, W1D 3QY

www.acblack.com

ISBN 978-1-4081-2450-5

A CIP catalogue for this book is available from the British Library.

This book is produced using paper that is made from wood grown in managed, sustainable forests. It is natural, renewable and recyclable. The logging and manufacturing processes conform to the environmental regulations of the country of origin.

Printed and bound in Great Britain
by CPI Cox & Wyman, Reading RG1 8EX.

Contents

1

Princess of Alexandria

Cleopatra's sister flung the senet board off the table. 'I'm not playing games with you any more,' she snapped. 'You cheat.'

'I do not cheat, Berenice,' Cleopatra said quietly. 'I win.' She was careful not to anger her sister. Berenice would be queen one day.

Cleopatra signalled to a servant, who picked up the board and collected the game pieces.

'I'm going outside,' said Berenice, turning away.

'Don't go into the city,' Cleopatra warned. 'There's been trouble. The people are angry. I don't know why.'

Berenice looked back, her face hard. 'Don't tell me what to do,' she said. Then she left the room, followed by her handmaid.

Cleopatra stood on the shady balcony and watched her sister stride along a path between rows of gushing fountains.

'Yes, you'll be queen one day,' she murmured to herself. 'But I would make a much better one than you. You are not clever. You're just greedy for power.'

Cleopatra's family were careful to protect their power. Her ancestor, King Ptolemy I, had been made pharaoh of Egypt in 305 BC, just 247 years before. He was from Macedonia and spoke Greek. All male children born to the kings were called Ptolemy, and every Ptolemy since had known how important it was to be firm and strong. There were many other rulers who would love to add Egypt to their empires. And they would especially love to get their hands on Alexandria, the magnificent city that was Cleopatra's home.

The princess wandered through the palace halls, wondering if it was too late to go to the library. She heard the sound of raised voices as she passed her father's private rooms.

'I am your pharaoh!' he shouted. 'Don't you *dare*

criticise my actions! I have only the good of Egypt at heart. You must know that.'

Cleopatra stopped to listen. She knew that many people did not approve of her father. He, Ptolemy Auletes, was known as 'The Flute Player', which made it sound as if he wasn't a serious king. But that wasn't true. He tried very hard to keep some sort of friendship between Egypt and powerful Rome, which already ruled many other lands. The Romans mustn't be allowed to conquer Egypt, too!

Cleopatra jumped back as her father's door flew open and his team of ministers burst out. They looked angry.

'The people can't be kept down for much longer,' muttered the chief of them, the vizier. 'There'll be trouble, you mark my words, and –' Catching sight of Cleopatra, he bowed. 'Your forgiveness, Princess.' He hurried along behind the other men, his face red.

Cleopatra stared after them. Her father was the king, Egypt's pharaoh – a *god*. No harm could come to him. It wasn't possible, was it?

2
A King in Fear

One morning shortly afterwards, Cleopatra watched the king dismiss his ministers and walk slowly, head down, into one of his private rooms. The year had been a troubled one for him, she knew, but she'd never seen her father quite so disturbed.

The princess took a deep breath. 'Wait here,' she whispered to her handmaid, and slipped inside, closing the door behind her.

'Father?'

'Eh? Oh, Cleopatra, my love.' King Ptolemy XII put his head in his hands and sighed.

Cleopatra waved his servants away, and poured him a cup of wine with her own hands.

'What's wrong, Father?' she asked gently.

He smiled sadly. 'It's complicated, little one.'

'You could tell me,' said Cleopatra. 'I know I'm only twelve, but I'll try to understand.'

The king took her hand. 'I *know* you will. You are the cleverest of my children. In fact, you are the cleverest child I know.' He sighed. 'I have done what I thought best for Egypt, but I have made mistakes.'

'Tell me,' Cleopatra murmured, knowing that he would give in to her. He always did.

King Ptolemy suggested they walk in the gardens while they talked, and Cleopatra readily agreed. She had learned long ago that it was safer to talk outside, where you couldn't be overheard by someone hiding in the shadows.

The sun shimmered low in the sky, and the air was cooling slightly. Part of the palace gardens overlooked the sea, and the seaweed-scented breeze was welcome.

'There are three men ruling Rome,' the king began, 'Pompey, Julius Caesar and Crassus.'

'And they are called the triumvirate.'

The king reached up, pulled a deep-pink flower

from a tree and presented it to her. 'Cleopatra, how do you know so much?'

The princess tucked the flower in her gold arm bangle. 'I know a lot because I study hard, and I listen and learn.' Unlike Berenice, she thought.

'Well, I told the men of the triumvirate that I would pay them a large sum of money. Huge. In exchange, they named me a friend and ally of the Roman people. That means they're happy for me to rule Egypt, and they won't invade us. Our country is safe. However, now I have to give them the money, and there just isn't enough.'

'Can't you tax our people and make them pay?' asked Cleopatra. 'It's for their safety, after all.'

The king frowned. 'I decided that would be wrong. The people can't afford higher taxes. Instead, I borrowed the money from a Roman moneylender called Rabirius. But now I don't know how I'm going to pay it back.' He was silent for a moment, then took her hand. 'Cleopatra, whatever they say about me, remember I did it for Egypt – for our royal house of Ptolemy.'

The princess had no chance to answer. A hail of stones came over the wall. There were shouts.

'Flute Player! The Romans have conquered your brother's island. Cyprus is theirs!'

'Flute Player! Your brother killed himself sooner than be paraded as a prisoner in Rome.'

'Why didn't you help him, Flute Player? Why didn't you stop the Romans? Are we going to be next?'

Loyal guards quickly surrounded the king and the princess and hurried them inside. While her father rushed to his advisers, Cleopatra ran to an upstairs window. Shielded by a filmy cream curtain, she watched the fighting on the quayside. Her stomach churned with fear.

'The people hate my father,' she said to her handmaid, Eiras.

'No, Highness, surely not,' said the girl, but Cleopatra could see she did not mean it.

The next day, the king was gone.

Cleopatra's family gathered with her father's ministers. These wise men explained that the king's life was threatened by the Egyptian people. They despised the things he'd done, and also things he hadn't done. They felt he should have helped his brother, rather than let the Romans take Cyprus for their own. Cyprus had, after all, belonged to Egypt.

Arsinoë, Cleopatra's younger sister, asked, 'Will our father come home?'

'Of course he will,' the vizier assured her. 'Just as soon as things settle down.'

'What about the money he owes?' asked Cleopatra.

Berenice glanced at her sharply.

The vizier paused. 'The money will be repaid,' he said, looking at the floor. 'Have no fear.'

Cleopatra's younger brothers, who were all called Ptolemy, took no notice of what was being said. They were itching to go out on the picnic they'd been promised.

'Highnesses,' said the vizier, 'while His Majesty is away, all will carry on as before.'

As she left, Cleopatra noticed that Berenice stayed behind to talk to the ministers. She soon found out why.

One morning shortly afterwards, a messenger came to Cleopatra's rooms and bowed. 'Highness, your sister commands you to come to her in the royal throne room.'

What on earth's she doing there? Cleopatra wondered. Aloud she said, 'Tell her I will come when I have bathed.'

She took her time, as always, over her bath. Once she was dressed, she slipped her feet into pale-blue jewelled sandals and made her way to the massive throne room. There, she found her brothers and Arsinoë once more, together with the vizier and other ministers. But this time they were all on their knees. They were on their knees in front of...

'Berenice!' Cleopatra gasped.

Her sister was wearing the crown of Egypt; their father's crown.

'Kneel, Cleopatra! Kneel before me, Berenice IV, Queen of Egypt!'

As Cleopatra sank slowly to her knees, her heart sank, too.

3
Queen of Egypt

Cleopatra and her brothers and younger sister could do nothing. Berenice had the support of important Egyptians and she was clearly a ruler to be feared, especially by those close to her. Soon after the new queen married her cousin in 57 BC, the poor man was dead.

'Cleopatra,' Arsinoë whispered as they ate breakfast together on a balcony overlooking the harbour, 'is it true Berenice had him murdered?'

Cleopatra nodded. 'Strangled. My tutor said she was always cross with him because he was nasty, and dirty. He hardly ever bathed.' She held her sister's hand. 'Don't be afraid, Arsinoë. Just take care not to make her angry.'

'But it's so easy to annoy her these days. I don't know what to do.'

Cleopatra chose a soft, ripe fig and offered it to Arsinoë. 'If we keep quiet and behave, she won't be unkind to us. She is our sister, after all. Anyway, she'll soon be busy choosing another husband. She can't rule alone.'

Arsinoë bit her fig and a piece of the deep-pink flesh dropped to the floor. She kicked it aside just as her maid bent to pick it up, and her toe gave the girl a blow on the elbow. 'Mind my foot!' she snapped.

Everyone seems cross these days, Cleopatra thought. She pulled Arsinoë to her feet and they wandered into the garden, nibbling almonds as they walked.

Slipping behind a bank of flowering pomegranate bushes, the sisters sat by a small pool while their handmaids waited in the hot sun. When the princesses were small, this had been their favourite place for sharing secrets.

'Arsinoë,' Cleopatra said, 'I don't want to raise your hopes, but I believe Father will return one day. He'll hear what Berenice has done, and he'll raise an army against her supporters. Then he'll come back to rule Egypt again.'

'And Berenice will be punished,' said Arsinoë. 'But when's that going to be? When will Father come home?'

Cleopatra didn't know. 'We must be patient,' she said.

They were patient for nearly two years, during which time Cleopatra occupied herself studying. She adored learning different languages, and practising her new skills on foreign visitors, though that didn't happen very often now the king was gone. He had loved showing off his clever little daughter. Berenice preferred to shine alone, but she'd never bothered to learn to speak Egyptian; none of the family had, except Cleopatra. Everyone who spoke with them had to speak Greek.

One day, Cleopatra was chatting to her tutor after lessons when she caught sight of Berenice's current husband, Archelaos. He was striding, red-faced and angry, through the courtyard below. He swore and lashed out at a gardener, who didn't see him in time to kneel and bow.

Cleopatra moved back into the shadows. 'What's Berenice done to him now?' she whispered to herself. 'If her supporters knew what a tyrant she is, they'd wish for my father's return, I know they would.'

Behind her, the tutor murmured. 'They might yet have that wish, if the gods will it.'

Cleopatra spun round. She'd forgotten he was there.

The man bowed. 'Forgive me, Highness. I spoke without thinking.'

'Stand straight,' Cleopatra ordered. 'Don't be afraid. We're old friends, aren't we? Tell me what you mean.'

The tutor glanced round, and put a finger to his lips.

'Of course,' said Cleopatra. 'Come. We'll walk on to the harbour. The sea air will clear our minds.'

Twenty minutes later, they stood on the private quayside, where only royal boats were moored. Cleopatra turned to her tutor. 'So tell me what you know and how you know it – and I want the truth.'

'I know someone who knows the wife of the

scribe to the vizier.'

Cleopatra smiled. 'Your wife is sister to that scribe's wife, I think!'

He gaped. 'How –?'

'I look and listen, and I keep my knowledge to myself. Now, tell me!' the princess commanded.

'Highness, your father knows that your sister has taken his place. He plans to return.'

Cleopatra clapped her hand over her mouth to stop herself from crying out.

'A Roman army will attack and win back the throne for him.'

'But he cannot pay the soldiers,' Cleopatra gabbled. 'Where will he get the money?'

The tutor shrugged. 'Borrow it?'

'Borrow *more*?' If my father owes the Romans too much, she thought, Rome will have an even greater claim on Egypt.

She promised the tutor she'd keep quiet about his wife and her friend passing on information. Privately, she vowed that in future she'd watch all those in positions of trust. They might seem to be loyal, but you never could tell. It paid to know what everyone was up to.

When the attack came, in 55 BC, it came from the east. King Ptolemy paid the Roman general, Gabinius, who was governor of Syria, to bring his army – the Gabinians – to conquer Alexandria. Berenice's husband was killed in the fighting, and she was taken prisoner.

Cleopatra, with her younger sister and brothers, kept to their rooms and waited. They were terrified of this foreign army. What would happen to them? Where was their father?

At night, they kept their servants and guards near, and tried hard to sleep. Although the Romans had won the battle, and were in charge of Alexandria, some Egyptians still refused to give in. Every time fighting broke out near the palace, the sea breezes carried the sound of men's angry cries and screams of pain into the royal bedrooms.

Within a few weeks, King Ptolemy returned to the palace. But it was not the homecoming Cleopatra had imagined. Her father had little time for his children. Instead, he spent hours arguing with the Gabinian leaders. He was livid, in a furious rage. In his absence, his throne had been taken from him, and his people had given their support to Berenice.

One Roman officer in particular, Mark Antony, tried to calm things down. 'Your people will hate you if you punish them,' he said.

'Someone must pay!' the king stormed.

Mark Antony suggested that the king should arrest Berenice and her ministers, but leave the people alone. 'In that way you'll win back their support,' he explained.

Cleopatra ordered her servants to find out everything they could. 'Make friends with the Gabinian officers,' she said. 'Ask them about Mark Antony. Give them fine food and lots of wine. Get them talking.'

'Mark Antony's so handsome,' Arsinoë remarked. 'And a great soldier.'

Cleopatra shrugged. 'He's a Roman. And if Father doesn't get things sorted out quickly, he could be our ruler one day!'

Fortunately, King Ptolemy *did* sort things out. He took all the property and belongings from the prisoners and used it to pay off some of his huge debt. Roman leaders agreed to let him rule Egypt again, but they left a Gabinian army in Alexandria for support.

Next, King Ptolemy ordered the execution of the people who had taken his throne. When Cleopatra and Arsinoë heard this, their thoughts flew to their imprisoned sister. Cleopatra asked to speak with the king.

'Father,' she said, 'will Berenice be kept prisoner for long?'

The king shook his head, his face grave. 'Not long, my love.'

'Then she'll return to us soon?'

Again, the king shook his head. 'Cleopatra, you are now heir to the throne of Egypt. One day you will be Queen.'

'But –' Like a thunderbolt, the truth hit her. 'Berenice is to be executed? She will die?'

'She's a threat to the peace of Egypt. While she lives, she could build up a new army of followers, and try to take the throne again. She *must* die.'

Cleopatra whirled away and ran through the palace halls. She flung herself on her bed, sobbing with grief … and fear.

4

Enemies at Work

King Ptolemy was pharaoh again, with Rome's support. He kept Cleopatra close by and taught her how important it was to keep a good relationship with the powerful Romans.

Rome and all its conquered lands had been ruled by Pompey, Julius Caesar and Crassus until Crassus was killed in battle. Pompey was married to Caesar's daughter, Julia, and the relationship between the two men had been excellent until Julia's death in 54 BC. After that, although they shared power, they didn't get on as friends.

Cleopatra made it her business to know all this, not just because it was her duty as a princess, but because she loved to learn.

King Ptolemy made sure that his relationship with Rome was good, but unfortunately his relationship with his own people was not. They were now taxed heavily because the king needed vast sums of money to pay off his debts, and this time he did not hesitate to demand it from them.

In 51 BC, four years after his return to power, King Ptolemy XII died. Poor Cleopatra had little time to grieve – the king's will stated that she must inherit his throne.

Cleopatra VII, aged just eighteen, was the new Queen of Egypt.

A young queen wasn't in a very strong position, but King Ptolemy had thought of that; his will also stated that Cleopatra must marry her young brother, Ptolemy XIII, and they would rule together. This wasn't at all unusual in Egyptian royal families.

'Aren't you afraid, Cleopatra?' Arsinoë asked when they had a moment to themselves. 'Aren't you scared of the Romans? They conquer every land they can. Surely they will now want to conquer Egypt.'

Cleopatra put an arm round her sister. 'Our father was clever, Arsinoë. He has made Rome the guardians of Ptolemy and myself. They'll protect us. He even sent a copy of his will to the great Roman triumvir, Pompey. No, I'm more afraid of dangers inside Egypt than of the Romans.'

Arsinoë curled up with her head in Cleopatra's lap. 'What dangers inside? Inside where?'

'Inside our own palace. Ptolemy is only ten, so he needs his own team of advisers, like a sort of council, to help him make good decisions. They're the people I fear most.'

Arsinoë looked up. 'Why?'

'All three men – his tutor Theodotos, the soldier Achillas and, most of all, Pothinus – would love to be rid of me, and of Rome. Then, through Ptolemy, they would have such power!'

The sisters hugged. 'Take care of yourself,' Arsinoë whispered. 'If you die, something bad might happen to me, too. Wear the uraeus whenever you're in public. It will watch over you.'

The uraeus, a headband with three rearing cobras, protected the crown of Egypt, and the pharaoh. And so it protected Cleopatra.

The new queen needed the Egyptians to love her. She made a long trip on the Nile by royal barge to show herself to the people. But the harvest was bad and the poor men who farmed along the Nile were unhappy, especially when they were ordered to send their spare crops to Alexandria, or face the punishment of death.

Cleopatra could understand their anger, but she was desperate to keep the people of Alexandria on her side. They would be the biggest danger to her if rioting began.

Then a crisis arose. Trouble was brewing between Pompey and Caesar, and Caesar marched on Rome. That meant war – Romans against Romans!

Pompey sent his son to ask the Egyptians for support – for soldiers, food and warships. He had helped King Ptolemy when he fled to Rome, and now he wanted the favour returned.

It was Pothinus who gave the order to supply Pompey's son with warships, soldiers and wheat to feed them. But the angry Egyptians blamed Cleopatra.

'Food going to foreigners when we're near starving!' they grumbled. 'What sort of a queen does she think she is?'

Pothinus took every opportunity to make Cleopatra appear bad in the eyes of the Egyptians. Soon, it seemed as if everyone was against her. The queen decided to leave the country while she could.

'Goodbye, darling Arsinoë,' she whispered at dawn one morning. 'I have to go. Who knows what Pothinus might do next? He wants me dead so he can rule Egypt through Ptolemy.'

'But what about me?' Arsinoë whimpered. 'Please don't leave.'

'I must. I fear for my life.' Cleopatra signalled to her servants and, in complete silence, they were gone.

An hour later, the queen stood on the deck of her great ship and watched as Alexandria disappeared from view. She watched until she could no longer see the fiery glow from the Pharos Island lighthouse.

'I'll be back,' she vowed. 'I'll raise an army and I'll return to rule once more. Watch out, Pothinus, you haven't seen the last of Queen Cleopatra.'

5
While the Queen's Away

Cleopatra might have fled, but she wasn't going to give up her throne lightly. If Ptolemy's scheming advisers would not allow her to rule alongside her brother, he must be deposed. Then she would deal with Pothinus – unmercifully.

She immediately set about keeping the vow she'd made to herself. Loyal Alexandrians joined Cleopatra and raised an army.

With the queen gone, the Roman senate agreed that Ptolemy XIII was now pharaoh of Egypt.

Pompey was still guardian of the young king, but he had huge worries of his own. In the summer of 48 BC, Julius Caesar had defeated Pompey's army in Greece, and had become the most powerful Roman of all. Now, weeks later, there was just one place that Pompey could go where he was confident of a warm welcome and support. He fled to Egypt, not realising that Cleopatra was already on her way to attack and take back Alexandria.

Once his boat was anchored near the palace, Pompey sent messengers ashore to get the news.

'King Ptolemy is at Pelusium, not far from here. It's east of Alexandria,' came the report, 'and he's camped there with his army of Gabinian soldiers, waiting for Cleopatra.'

'He's gone to meet his sister? I thought they were enemies.'

'They are, sir,' said the messenger. 'Cleopatra has gathered her own army and is marching this way. King Ptolemy hopes to defeat her in battle before she reaches Alexandria.'

Pompey thought about the situation. He was in trouble. He'd come to be protected from Caesar, who was surely following him with a fleet of warships, but there was hardly any Roman army left in Alexandria to help him. He needed to speak to Ptolemy, urgently.

'Go to Pelusium,' he ordered the messenger.

'Ask if the king will see me.'

When the message was delivered that evening, King Ptolemy's advisers went into a huddle round their camp fire. What should they tell the young king to do? What was the best plan? If they refused to help, and Pompey sailed off, they'd have made a bad enemy. Worse, Caesar would turn up and find Pompey had evaded him. Then he'd be angry with the Egyptian leaders for letting his enemy slip away.

'I've thought of something else,' said Achillas, the soldier. 'Pompey might sail along the coast to join Cleopatra's army. Remember, we told everyone it was *her* who gave warships and food to him? He'd be glad to fight on her side.'

Theodotos tossed a chunk of wood on the fire, scattering ash. 'Pompey's already lost one battle against Caesar, and he's not likely to survive another,' he said. 'We really ought to make *friends* with Caesar. We could do with his help in getting rid of Cleopatra.'

'Good thinking,' said Pothinus. 'And I have just the plan. Achillas, if you do as I say, Caesar will be so grateful to King Ptolemy that *he'll* be Egypt's friend and protector from now on. We won't need Pompey any more.' He stirred the fire with a stick, sending sparks rocketing into the night air.

'Excellent!' said Achillas. 'What's your idea?'

'We kill Pompey.'

A few days later, a fleet of Roman warships sailed towards the harbour at Alexandria. When Julius Caesar stepped ashore, Theodotos and Pothinus greeted him with great ceremony. After they'd spoken politely for a few minutes, Pothinus said, 'Great Caesar, we have two gifts for you.'

Caesar liked presents. 'How intriguing,' he said.

First, Pothinus presented the Roman general with a ring.

Caesar examined it. 'This looks like Pompey's ring! Where did you –?'

Pothinus' servant came forward and knelt, offering Caesar a large covered earthenware pot.

'What's this?' asked Caesar. 'Egyptian gold? Or merely figs!' He laughed.

Pothinus lifted the lid. He reached inside the pot, grasped the contents and held it up.

The watching Romans gasped. Julius Caesar turned pale. Pothinus was holding, by its hair, the head of Pompey.

Caesar's anger shocked Pothinus. 'He may have been my enemy, but for years he was my friend. A great man. He didn't deserve to die like this!'

Pothinus was afraid to speak.

Caesar turned away, touched Pompey's ring to his lips and buried his face in his hands. He stood for a few moments, his shoulders shuddering, then he took a deep breath. 'Now … you,' he said to Pothinus' servant, 'lead me to the palace. I have work to do. I'm going to settle the trouble between King Ptolemy and Queen Cleopatra as Pompey would have done, and they will rule as their father wished. And speaking of their father,' he added as he strode away, 'I have a large debt to collect.'

Pothinus' teeth were clenched. 'If he thinks he can put Cleopatra back on the throne, he'll have to think again.'

Theodotos was still shaken by Caesar's reaction to their gift. 'He'll station his men here. They'll eat our food and drink our wine. What right do they have to do that?'

'Come, Theodotos,' said Pothinus. 'Let's go to the palace. We can pretend to do what Caesar demands. We can pretend to welcome the Romans to Alexandria. We can supply food to his army.' He smiled. 'But it doesn't have to be good food. We'll give them wheat for bread, of course. But it will be rotten wheat. Wheat that's got damp, that rats have scurried over and left droppings in – filthy wheat that will turn their Roman stomachs.'

Theodotos smiled as they reached the cool palace entrance. 'And we'll send men into the city to stir up hatred of the Romans. Alexandria will be in turmoil. Caesar will see that there's nothing here for him, and he'll go.'

'Leaving us to help our young king rule Egypt.'

They both chuckled.

'We'll soon hold power again, Theodotos,' said Pothinus. 'Don't you worry.'

6
Homecoming

'Eiras!' Cleopatra called her handmaiden. 'He's sent for me! Julius Caesar wants me to go to Alexandria. He says it's for my benefit, and that he's said nothing of my visit to my brother or his advisers.'

'Mistress, don't go,' said Eiras. 'The moment you set foot in Alexandria, soldiers from your brother, the king, will arrest you.'

Cleopatra bit her lip. 'You're right,' she said. 'I'll think while I eat. Give me my mirror.' She nibbled some slivers of cold roast goose and gazed into the mirror's polished silver surface for a while, then she slapped it down on the table, making Eiras jump.

'Has Apollodorus arrived?' Cleopatra asked.

'The merchant Apollodorus?' Eiras looked

puzzled. 'Yes, I believe so. He's brought some goods you ordered for your army. But why –'

'Hush, girl! Ask him to dine with me.'

Eiras glanced at the other servants. 'If you wish, Highness,' she said in a disapproving tone.

Cleopatra glared at her. 'I do wish. Now fetch Charmion to arrange my hair.'

Two hours later, Cleopatra sat facing Apollodorus. He looked uncomfortable at being allowed to sit in her presence. To him, she was the mighty Queen of Egypt.

'Apollodorus, you've known my family for many years, and you've served us well. My father thought highly of you. Will you now do something for me?'

Apollodorus slid off his seat, knelt and touched his forehead to Cleopatra's golden sandal. 'Anything, Highness.'

'You will obey me without question?'

Apollodorus said proudly, 'I am yours to command, and will obey.'

Cleopatra smiled. 'Good friend, you may feel differently when I tell you what I have in mind.'

A week later, Apollodorus' ship lay at anchor off the coast near Alexandria, a rowing boat bobbing against its side. The merchant and Cleopatra were alone on deck. Their destination was pinpointed by the flare of the Pharos lighthouse.

Cleopatra shivered, though the night was warm.

'I'll send for your maid, Highness,' said Apollodorus. 'She can fetch you a cloak.'

The queen shook her head. 'No need. I'll soon be wrapped up warmly enough.'

Apollodorus shook his head, 'Please, Highness –'

Cleopatra touched a finger to his lips. 'Hush. You promised to obey me. You have the bed linen?'

He showed her where thick layers of white linen lay spread on the deck, like a bed. Beside them was a long narrow bag with a drawstring top.

Cleopatra stroked the fine cloth. 'It will be soft against my skin.' She lay down on the linen. 'Don't drop me, Apollodorus.'

'I'll guard you with my life.' The merchant took the edge of the linen and folded it over the queen's body, then gently rolled it up, with her inside.

'I'll slide the bag over you now, Highness, but

I'll tie it only loosely at the top. You'll have plenty of air.'

When it was done, Apollodorus lifted the precious bundle. 'Hey! You below!' he called to his men. 'Help me over the side and into the boat. I have a gift for Julius Caesar.'

As Apollodorus rowed ashore, Cleopatra concentrated on breathing deeply. She was terrified the movement of the little boat might make her sick.

'We're approaching the harbour,' whispered Apollodorus.

'The guards will challenge you,' the bundle replied. 'Show them my gold scarab ring, then they will let you pass.'

A few minutes later, Cleopatra heard the guards try to protest, then Apollodorus' deep voice saying, 'I come on the queen's business, with a gift for Caesar.'

Cleopatra felt sure the guards would hear her heart thumping but, after some hurried discussion, they told Apollodorus to pass. She felt herself being lifted and carried up the steps onto the harbour wall.

'Keep quiet, Highness,' Apollodorus whispered. 'A guard is leading the way.'

Cleopatra was so nervous she could hardly breathe. It seemed an age until she heard Apollodorus' name being announced to Caesar. She strained to hear what they were saying, but Apollodorus had shifted her from his shoulder to lie across his arms; the linen pressed against her ears, muffling any sound.

At last, Cleopatra sensed herself being lowered gently to the floor. She felt hands at the neck of the bag, untying the leather thong. Then Apollodorus shifted her body gently and slid off the bag. Now she could hear again.

A strange voice said, 'Linen? Queen Cleopatra sends a gift of linen?'

She shivered. It was the voice of Julius Caesar!

Apollodorus spoke. 'Egyptian linen is the finest. Very precious. Shall I unroll it, Caesar?'

'No,' was the reply. 'Let me take a look first.'

Cleopatra felt a nudge, and guessed she was being poked by a foot.

'It's certainly the finest linen I've ever seen,' said Caesar. 'I'd like to see if it's as good all the way to the centre of the roll.' He paused. 'I'll just grip the edges and ... there!'

Without warning, Cleopatra felt herself spinning and bumping across the marble floor until there was a burst of light. She was free.

With as much dignity as possible, Cleopatra, Queen of Egypt, rose, brushed herself down, and faced Julius Caesar, the mighty Roman general. She glared at him. 'Are you laughing at me?'

Caesar raised his hands. 'No, Highness, merely smiling.'

She continued to glare.

'Smiling with delight at such beauty,' he said.

'Oh.' Cleopatra walked to a chair and sat, head high.

Apollodorus stood by the door, beside the Roman guards.

Caesar ordered refreshments, and when Cleopatra had relaxed a little after her strange journey, she said, 'You sent for me. Why?'

'I intend to make sure that your father's will is honoured. His wish was that you and your brother should rule Egypt together. I'm going to make that happen.'

'Excellent.' Cleopatra smiled at the tall, well-dressed Roman. 'That's my wish, too.'

Caesar leaned forward and looked straight into her eyes. 'But we both know someone who has other ideas.'

Cleopatra sipped her wine, feeling very satisfied. Her brother, Ptolemy, was in for quite a shock. And as for Pothinus...

7
A New Beginning

Caesar was impressive. He was much older than Cleopatra – nearly three times her age. What hair he had was cut neatly, and he looked well dressed and fresh. She'd heard he had a good sense of humour and that men admired him. Women admired him, too. Caesar was already on his third marriage, to a noblewoman called Calpurnia, but Cleopatra knew she was far away in Rome.

'Calpurnia's probably twice my age,' she thought that night as she climbed into her own bed in the palace once again. 'Old, really. I'm young and beautiful. I'll make Caesar like me. I'll make him want to stay in Alexandria, to protect me from Ptolemy's advisers. He has great power.' She snuggled down under the sheet. 'I like powerful men.'

Cleopatra found it hard to sleep. She thought over the hours of conversation she'd had with Caesar that evening. How he'd told her of his sadness when his daughter, Julia, died.

'I understand your feelings so well,' Cleopatra had said, reaching out to touch his arm. 'My own sister is dead.'

Now, going over the conversation, she felt her own loss was worse. After all, Berenice had been killed, whereas Julia had merely been ill. Anyway, Caesar could always have another daughter.

Cleopatra thought how surprised Arsinoë would be when she saw her in the morning. She finally fell asleep trying to picture the shock on her husband-brother's face.

At dawn, Cleopatra rose early and considered her situation while she bathed.

'Send for Eiras and Charmion,' she told the handmaid who attended her, 'but not yet. Speak to no one until I've spoken with Caesar.' For she knew she would.

Sure enough, minutes later, the handmaid was called to speak to a messenger. She returned and said, 'Highness, Caesar invites you to break your fast with him.'

'When?'

'At your leisure, the messenger said.'

Cleopatra stepped out of her bath and was wrapped in soft white cloth. She gripped the handmaid's arm. 'Are you sure the messenger said, "Caesar invites Queen Cleopatra?" He didn't say, "Caesar *summons* Queen Cleopatra?"'

'Yes, Highness, he said "invites".'

Cleopatra smiled. Summoned one day, invited the next. Things were changing. She spun round. 'Dry me, girl! Hurry!'

An hour later, she checked her green eye makeup in a polished silver mirror, then peered into the jewellery box the girl held for her. She chose a simple diadem of gold and lapis lazuli, a gold bracelet to snake around each arm, and a pair of matching turquoise rings. The handmaid finished Cleopatra's hair once the diadem was in place and finally she was ready.

Caesar greeted Cleopatra, looking deep into her eyes. They were barely seated when there was a commotion outside, the doors flew open and

Arsinoë burst in.

'I didn't believe them!' She threw herself at her sister's feet. 'My servants said you were back ... I dared not believe it. But you are!'

Cleopatra took her sister's hand and hugged her. 'I'm glad to see you, Arsinoë,' said Cleopatra. 'So is our guest.'

Caesar raised an eyebrow at being called 'guest', but Arsinoë didn't notice. 'I beg your pardon,' she said. 'I'm just so happy to see my sister unharmed. If I may, Cleopatra, I'll visit you later.' Head held high, she left.

Caesar and Cleopatra had barely begun to eat the apricots, peaches and golden-crusted honey bread set before them when they heard loud voices.

'Aha! My next, er ... guest,' said Caesar. 'Your husband.'

Cleopatra caught her breath. She intended to enjoy this moment.

The doors opened and Ptolemy stalked in. He stopped dead at the sight of Cleopatra sitting with the man who'd practically taken over his own palace.

The shock on Ptolemy's face was extremely satisfying for his sister.

'Cleopatra! It's true! You're back!' He turned to Caesar. 'I had my servant whipped for saying she'd returned. Why was I not told?'

'Why indeed?' Caesar murmured.

Cleopatra stood up. 'I'll tell you why! If your advisers had known I was coming, I wouldn't have been allowed to reach the palace gates alive.'

Ptolemy flushed. 'I don't know what you mean.'

Caesar spread his arms. 'Please. Be seated. I have lots to say to you both.'

Ptolemy flopped onto the nearest seat, but Cleopatra walked gracefully back to her chair. As she sat, she glanced at Caesar and smiled, thinking, he can barely take his eyes off me.

Both sister and brother listened until Caesar had finished speaking. Then Ptolemy said, 'Are you – a Roman – asking that I allow my sister to rule jointly with me?'

'No,' said Caesar. 'I'm *insisting* that you do.'

Ptolemy leapt up and stamped his foot in temper. 'Why should I?'

'Because our father –' Cleopatra began, but

Caesar laid a hand on hers. She kept still. She found herself enjoying the great man's gentle touch.

'Joint rule was your father's wish,' said Caesar. 'It's as simple as that. And I'm now calling your ministers, advisers and nobles together. I'll read your father's will aloud, so there can be no doubt. I'll call upon them all to support you both.'

Ptolemy folded his arms and stuck out his bottom lip.

Cleopatra felt ashamed that her brother – a king – still behaved like a child.

'So,' said Caesar, 'do you agree?'

'I do,' Cleopatra said sweetly. 'Ptolemy? Will you rule with me?'

He sniffed. 'Suppose so.'

'Good!' said Caesar. 'Then let's arrange this meeting.'

'And afterwards,' said Cleopatra, 'a banquet! To celebrate peace – between us all!'

Cleopatra barely listened as Caesar addressed the great men of Alexandria. She was intently watching the faces of Ptolemy's advisers. They sat on stools, glowering, near Ptolemy's throne. At one point, she caught Pothinus' eye. It took all her strength of will to hold his gaze until he looked away. But hold it she did.

'You're still my enemy,' she thought. 'But I am strong.' She glanced towards Caesar, thinking he looked more of a king than Ptolemy. 'And now I have a strong new friend.'

8
The Trouble With Sisters

Cleopatra was delighted to be back on the throne, and to have Caesar as her ally. She wasn't pleased at having to share the kingdom with Ptolemy, but she did her best to show Caesar how co-operative she could be. She needed to keep his friendship, so she told her servants, 'Do everything to make this banquet one Caesar will never forget. We must show him how respected he is.'

Cleopatra took hours getting ready and, when satisfied that she looked her most radiant, she made her entrance.

Caesar was enchanted by the glamour of the occasion. Lamplight glittered on gold and silver; musicians, dancers and acrobats entertained the guests, and luxurious food came in a constant stream. But what enchanted Caesar most of all was the beautiful young queen. She was happy and fun. And with him at her side, Cleopatra felt safe. She couldn't resist a triumphant look at Pothinus.

Little did she know, at that moment, her brother's smiling chief adviser was plotting against her.

Pothinus' plan was simple. Caesar had only a small army – scarcely big enough to be called an army, really. Pothinus would secretly organise the return of Ptolemy's much larger Gabinian army, and tell the Alexandrian people to arm themselves and their slaves. They'd get rid of Caesar, kill Cleopatra, and Ptolemy would be left to rule alone.

Unfortunately for Pothinus, things weren't that easy. When the Egyptian army attacked, later in 48 BC, Caesar immediately set his men to guard the palace, and sent for reinforcements. He made sure that Cleopatra, King Ptolemy, Arsinoë and their younger brother were kept safely inside. Cleopatra was glad of his protection, but worried sick that the Gabinian soldiers, under Achillas'

orders, would easily defeat Caesar's army. How long would it be before reinforcements arrived? Could they hold out until then?

They could and they did. Battle raged on land and sea – Alexandrians versus Romans. The city suffered. Homes, shops and businesses were burnt or destroyed. Lives were lost. No one was safe.

Clearly this battle was going to go on for some time. Caesar forbade the royal family from leaving the palace. Arsinoë and King Ptolemy were furious, but an armed Roman guard followed them everywhere. Cleopatra tried to convince her brothers and sister that they were better off under Caesar's protection, but King Ptolemy whined to be allowed to meet with his three advisers.

'If you leave, you won't last five minutes,' she told them. 'Go into the gardens and listen. There's fighting and hatred everywhere.'

Even though Cleopatra defended Caesar to her brother and sister, she herself was outraged when Caesar set fire to the Egyptian fleet. She watched from the palace windows as burning torches were flung onto ship after ship. The harbour was a sea of flame.

'My fine fleet!' she raged to Eiras and Charmion, although in her heart she knew that Caesar must win if she was going to keep her throne.

Charmion was cleaning Cleopatra's dressing table. She took a comb to a side window, pulled hairs from it, and let them drift away on the strong breeze. Suddenly, she gasped. 'Highness! The wind's changed. The fire's spreading to the land!'

Cleopatra ran to the window. Her knees went weak. 'The library,' she whispered. 'Oh, gods, not the library…' She ran from the room, but was stopped by her guards.

'Highness, our orders are to keep you here, safe.'

'The library's burning! Get out of my way!'

Charmion and Eiras did their best to calm Cleopatra, while the guards assured her that the fire was being put out. 'Not much will be lost,' said one. 'Anyway, Highness, it's only books.'

She looked at him coldly. 'Only books?'

He nodded. 'That's all.'

Seconds later, he stared in shock, his cheek turning red where Queen Cleopatra had hit him as hard as she could.

'Fool!' she cried. 'The whole learning of the

world is in that building! It's the greatest library in the –'

She was interrupted by joyful shouts from below. Hurrying to a window, she saw a Roman officer stagger and fall. His right arm was torn and bleeding. He stretched his other arm up towards the queen.

'Caesar is on Pharos Island!' he cried. 'Caesar controls the harbour.'

Cleopatra thanked the soldier and turned away. Would this war never end?

Late one evening, a few weeks later, while Caesar talked battle tactics with his officers, Cleopatra had an unexpected visitor.

'Arsinoë! I haven't seen you for ages.' Cleopatra hugged her. 'I know you hate being cooped up, but you know it's for our safety. Soon Caesar will win –' She felt Arsinoë stiffen. 'What?'

'Sister, we don't know he'll win. Our Egyptians are more than a match for him. If you'd only –'

Cleopatra held Arsinoë at arm's length and spoke firmly. 'Don't try to tell me what to do.

I have chosen Caesar as my friend and ally and I have complete faith in him.'

Arsinoë scowled. 'I think you'd like him to be more than a friend.'

Cleopatra's look would have terrified a servant, but her sister was unafraid. 'Arsinoë, don't you see, Rome would be a dreadful enemy to have? We need Caesar on our side.'

'I think you're half in love with him,' Arsinoë said slyly.

Cleopatra pushed her away. 'You're just a child. You know nothing of love – or war. Now leave me.'

Arsinoë smiled slightly. 'I will do exactly as you wish. Goodbye, sister. Think of me. Goodbye.'

At the time, Cleopatra took no notice of Arsinoë's words. She whiled away long hot days reading and studying, and spent her evenings dining and drinking with Caesar. She'd grown to enjoy his company. He, in turn, enjoyed her intelligence and charm. In the midst of war, they spent peaceful time together. Arsinoë was right about one thing, she thought. I *am* half in love with him.

Then one day towards the end of 48 BC, a messenger brought some peace-shattering news.

He knelt, head bowed, trembling.

'Are you afraid to speak, man?' Caesar snapped. 'Come, tell me what you have to say. No harm shall come to you.'

The messenger raised his head. 'The Princess Arsinoë hasn't been seen for many days. We searched all the palaces, but couldn't find her. Then we heard from one of mighty Caesar's spies –'

'Well? What of my sister? Speak, man!' Cleopatra interrupted.

'The princess was helped by Ganymedes –' the man began.

Caesar looked at Cleopatra.

'Her tutor,' she explained.

'Go on,' said Caesar.

'Ganymedes took her to join Achillas and the Egyptian army.'

Cleopatra gasped.

The messenger bowed his head again. 'Princess Arsinoë has declared herself Qu– Queen.'

9

The End of Two Enemies

Cleopatra was afraid. 'Caesar says the Alexandrian people support Arsinoë,' she moaned. 'They don't want me.'

Eiras stroked her mistress' hand. They'd been together for many years, and she could usually calm the queen.

But not this time.

Cleopatra snatched her hand away, and strode about the room. 'She cannot rule while I'm alive, Eiras. And that means she can only be planning one thing.'

'Surely she wouldn't have you killed, Highness,' said Eiras, shocked. 'Her own sister?'

Cleopatra spun round. 'Why not?' she

demanded. 'My father murdered his own daughter. Why would Arsinoë not kill me?'

Eiras turned pale.

'I must see Caesar,' Cleopatra snapped. 'Now!' She whirled from the room.

Moments later, she burst into the group of Roman officers surrounding Caesar. The great general looked at her coldly. 'We're speaking about war matters,' he said.

'And *I* wish to speak of more important things.' Cleopatra jerked her head at the Romans, as if to say 'get out'.

Caesar gave them the slightest of nods, and they left. Then he allowed Cleopatra to pour out her anger over Arsinoë's treachery. At last, she sank onto a chair and put her head in her hands. She was furious with herself for letting Caesar see her so afraid. But Caesar's next words surprised her.

'I fear assassination, too, Cleopatra,' he said. 'And remember – they must kill me to get to you.'

Cleopatra was grateful to hear this, but she knew an assassin didn't need to show him or herself by attacking with a dagger or sword. Death could be quiet and stealthy, perhaps by a poisoned peach, or a deadly snake or scorpion slipped into a bed.

Her thoughts were broken as an officer entered.

'What news?' said Caesar.

'We have them, sir.'

Cleopatra looked from one to the other. What were they talking about?

'Lock them up,' Caesar ordered.

The Roman hesitated. 'Both of them, sir?'

Caesar looked grim. 'Both. The king, too.'

The officer left.

Cleopatra walked slowly towards Caesar. 'I dislike my brother – my husband – as you well know, but I won't permit you – a *Roman* – to lock him up. He is the king, after all.'

Caesar grasped her elbow and pulled her to a balcony. 'Somewhere out there,' he said, 'your sister plots against you. Ptolemy and that toad, Pothinus, have been caught escaping, trying to join her. Cleopatra, they *all* plot against you. The only person who truly has your welfare at heart is me – as you say, a Roman. And my barber.'

'Your *barber*?'

'It was he who told me of their plans.'

'Reward him,' said Cleopatra. 'As for Pothinus...' She turned her back. 'Execute him.'

The queen had satisfaction at last. Hated Pothinus would never trouble her again.

Cleopatra raged to her women. 'How can those Alexandrian idiots accept Arsinoë – a *girl* – while I, their true queen, am trapped in my own palace, guarded by foreigners!' She paced up and down. 'How long must I put up with this? Why doesn't Caesar do something?'

Soon the battle took a surprising turn. Caesar's spies reported that Arsinoë had had a series of spectacular quarrels with her general, Achillas. She, a young girl, dealt with this situation in the way she thought best. It seemed simple. If Achillas disagreed with her, he must go. Ganymedes was ordered to kill him.

With Achillas gone, Ganymedes was put in charge of the army. Cleopatra was delighted. Not only was a second enemy, Achillas, dead, but Arsinoë's army was being run by her tutor.

'Who'd rate Ganymedes' chances against

Caesar?' she laughed. 'My sister's army is finished!'

But it wasn't. Ganymedes turned out to have a crafty streak in him. Caesar shook his head in admiration when he heard the news. 'That tutor is no fool,' he told Cleopatra. 'Guess what the man's done! He's fouled the water in the cisterns.'

'Cisterns?'

Caesar smiled. 'I suppose you think that fresh water just appears when you want it.'

Cleopatra shrugged. 'Well, it does, doesn't it?' Then she laughed. 'I know all about cisterns. Hundreds of them are dotted around the city – giant underground tanks, full of fresh water for Alexandria.'

'Not any more,' Caesar said grimly. 'Ganymedes gave orders for salt water to be let into the cisterns. The fresh water's ruined. There's nothing to drink except wine and beer. I've ordered teams of men to work around the clock, digging, until they find fresh water.'

To Cleopatra's joy, the angry people of Alexandria soon got fed up with Arsinoë and Ganymedes.

They felt the government under Arsinoë was unstable, and declared they'd rather have their king, Ptolemy, back than put up with Ganymedes' cruel laws.

'I trust young Ptolemy, you know,' Caesar told Cleopatra. 'He's changed a good deal since he's been held captive here. He, too, wants an end to war. I'll release him. That'll please the people.'

The queen was appalled. How could this great general be so stupid?

'He'll join his army,' Caesar continued. 'And of course he'll have to deal with Arsinoë and Ganymedes, but he's their rightful leader. The people will see he no longer wants to fight me, and there'll be peace in Egypt once again.'

It was no surprise to Cleopatra that as soon as her crafty brother reached his army, he turned round and set his sights on Alexandria, and the Roman who occupied his palace.

But Caesar was a highly experienced soldier. When he was offered help from friendly foreign kings, he sailed along the coast and met with them *behind* Ptolemy's army. Ptolemy was taken completely by surprise, and in a short time his army was defeated.

After the battle, a tired and hungry Caesar returned to dine with Cleopatra. 'Your throne is safe,' he said.

'And my sister?'

'Safe,' he said. 'My prisoner, of course, but safe.'

Cleopatra's face hardened. 'And my brother – my husband?'

Caesar took her hand. 'I'm sorry, dearest. Ptolemy fell into the river.'

'But he swims. He reached the shore?'

'I'm sorry,' Caesar repeated. 'His armour was too heavy. He drowned.'

Cleopatra closed her eyes, picturing her young brother in his armour, gleaming gold. She'd never see him again.

'Then I am undisputed queen,' she breathed. Turning sharply to Caesar, she asked, 'You have his body?'

'We don't. He was washed away.' Caesar poured wine for them both. 'But we have his armour; it was salvaged from the river.'

Cleopatra slipped off her sandals and curled up contentedly. 'Well, we won't think of him now.

We shan't think of anything to do with wars, or soldiers, or kings or queens.'

Caesar came to stand before her. 'I'm afraid we must. You're a widow. You need a new husband.'

10

Holidays and Celebrations

The obvious choice for a new husband was Cleopatra's 13-year-old brother, Ptolemy XIV. He had no poisonous advisers to threaten the safety of her throne, so Cleopatra was satisfied with him and, in 47 BC, they were married.

She now had a large army to keep the peace, so Caesar could have gone back to Rome. But he loved being with Cleopatra and she loved having him in Alexandria, so he stayed. Long, lazy, hot days were followed by evening entertainments and lots of feasting. They'd often stay up all night enjoying the company of friends. Mostly, they enjoyed each other's company.

Because Cleopatra loved Julius Caesar, she

wanted her people to love him, too. After all, they were close allies.

'We're going on a journey,' she announced one day. 'We'll travel up the River Nile, and we'll show ourselves off to my people. I want them to know that Rome is Egypt's true friend.'

Caesar was used to action and adventure, so he was glad to do something more interesting than loll around the palace. Cleopatra's barge was huge and grand. It had rooms on different levels, with plenty of space for the crew and all the attendants the couple needed. Hundreds of smaller ships sailed alongside it. Wherever they stopped, the queen invited important local people to feasts and entertainments. She needed all of Egypt to support her.

How different this journey was from the one she'd made as a new queen, when the people were suffering from poor harvests and resented paying heavy taxes! Cleopatra loved to see the effect her glittering floating palace had on the ordinary folk who lived and farmed along the banks of the Nile. Work stopped and fishing nets drooped as they stared in awe at the spectacle. The queen! Their queen! And what if her lover was a Roman? Better to be the Romans' friend than their enemy. And when this queen spoke, everyone could understand her! None of her ancestors had ever bothered to learn the Egyptians' language.

Cleopatra delighted in the attention. She enjoyed watching men hunting crocodiles and dangerous hippos, and others working and relaxing on the river. She and Caesar tried a little fishing, and he often swam with his officers.

Eventually, they turned for home. Caesar started to feel guilty that he'd stayed with Cleopatra for so long. He ought to return to his soldier's life. There were battles to be fought and won. But before he left, Cleopatra had a surprise for him.

One evening, they were having supper alone. When they'd finished, Cleopatra sent the servants away.

'Great Caesar,' she said, 'I have something to tell you. We're going to have a baby!' She laughed at his expression. 'If it's a boy, my love, he'll be called Ptolemy Caesar and one day he will rule Egypt. My country and Rome will always be friends.'

Caesar was delighted, and thrilled that his own

son would one day, as the true son of the Egyptian queen, be King! But in spite of Cleopatra's pleading, he didn't change his plans to go back to war.

The queen held her head high as her beloved Caesar left. She must never let ordinary people see her cry. After all, in their eyes, she was a goddess.

But when he'd gone, Cleopatra went to her bedroom. She had thousands of soldiers and servants and advisers, and even a boy-husband. But she'd never felt so alone.

She rested her hands over her bump, and smiled. Soon she wouldn't be quite so alone. She would have a baby to love!

When Ptolemy Caesar was born in the summer of 47 BC, his proud mother didn't want him to be known by the same name as the king. 'I'll call you Caesarion,' she said. 'My little Caesar.'

The baby's father was gone for over a year. Cleopatra wished he'd return, but she knew his work was important.

While he was away, Eiras and Charmion, her

favourite handmaids, became used to their mistress chattering on about Caesar.

'I hear news from Rome of wild celebrations,' she told them one day. 'He's won battles in Gaul and Africa and Asia, and I don't know where else! Isn't he amazing?'

'Amazing, Highness,' said Eiras. 'Little Caesarion will be so proud of his daddy when he's old enough to understand.'

Cleopatra sighed. 'I wish I could share the festivities with him. Imagine the processions, the parties and feasts!'

Charmion smiled. 'They're probably almost as grand as our Egyptian celebrations.'

However, there was one piece of news the queen didn't share with her handmaids. It was the Roman tradition to display important prisoners to the people. Usually these were men, but in this instance, there was a girl amongst them – Cleopatra's sister, Arsinoë. Even though she'd acted very badly, it was considered wrong to shame a royal princess in public.

The Romans thought so, too. Once Caesar got wind that his people thought it was cruel to treat a young princess like that, he tried to put things right by sparing Arsinoë's life. Instead of execution, she was banished to live in the temple of Artemis at Ephesus, across the sea.

In spite of what had happened in the past, Cleopatra couldn't help feeling pity for Arsinoë in her humiliation. But she soon put her sister out of her mind and carried on with life, all the time waiting and hoping for Caesar's return.

'When will he come?' she grumbled one day, as she wallowed in her bath.

'Soon, Highness, I'm sure,' Eiras said soothingly, adding more milk to the water.

'Soon?' Cleopatra slapped the water with the flat of her hand, splashing Eiras. 'What do you know?' she stormed. 'How can you know the mind of a Roman?' She sat up. 'You may wash my back.'

Cleopatra waited and waited, hoping for Caesar to return. Then one day she had a brilliant idea. If Caesar wouldn't come to Cleopatra, Cleopatra would go to Caesar!

'Ladies,' she announced to Charmion and Eiras. 'Prepare for a journey. We're going to Rome!'

There was such excitement in the palace.

Messages were sent to Caesar and, at long last, he replied.

'He's letting us stay in his finest house,' Cleopatra told Charmion and Eiras. She swept Caesarion out of his nursemaid's arms and danced around the room. 'You'll soon meet your daddy, little one, and all Rome will adore us!'

11

Life and Death in Rome

The weather was perfect when the Egyptian royal party arrived in Rome in the autumn of 46 BC. Although Cleopatra would rather have gone straight to Caesar's house, she knew there'd be a formal public welcome for them.

'We have to do this, darling,' she murmured to Caesarion. 'Egyptian royalty must occasionally be seen by the people, otherwise how can they love us?'

To her grumbling husband-brother, she said, 'I know you're tired, Ptolemy. We all are. But do *try* to look like a king.'

Once all the formalities were over, Caesar took the royal party to his magnificent riverside villa.

He led Cleopatra into a room away from everyone else, and kissed her tenderly. 'It's wonderful to see you again,' he whispered. 'Now, where's my son?'

Cleopatra laughed and clapped her hands. A smiling Eiras brought Caesarion in, and put him in his father's arms.

This was the beginning of a fantastic Roman holiday for Cleopatra. A round of feasts and entertainments began. Important Romans, keen to please Caesar, took the opportunity to entertain him and the queen he loved. His wife, Calpurnia, was used to Caesar having other lovers, and the great general had the excuse that it was important for him to entertain a foreign ruler.

Sadly, it couldn't last. One day, Caesar gave Cleopatra upsetting news. 'I'm leaving you for a while, my love,' he said. 'I must be a soldier again, and lead my army.'

'Where?' she asked sulkily.

'Spain,' he said. 'But before I go, I have something that will please you.' He took her to a new temple he'd had built in the forum.

Cleopatra was not impressed. 'I've seen it already,' she said. 'This is your temple to the goddess Venus. Do you think I'm pleased to see it again? I'm not.'

'Come inside,' said Caesar.

Cleopatra wouldn't make a fuss in public, so she did as she was asked. Beside the statue of the Roman goddess Venus, there was another statue.

'It's my goddess, Isis,' she cried in delight, 'and she's holding her son, Horus.'

'Look closer,' said Caesar.

Cleopatra gasped. 'Her face! It's –'

Caesar smiled. 'Her face is your face.'

'But your people will be angry to see a statue of an Egyptian queen in a Roman temple! They'll hate me!'

Caesar shook his head. 'This is a statue of Isis. Rome is linked to Egypt now, so the people will accept an Egyptian goddess, and respect her.'

'As I respect *your* gods,' said Cleopatra.

'Exactly.'

They returned to Caesar's villa, and he continued preparations for his journey.

At last the day came when Cleopatra stood proudly with Caesarion, as the man she loved left Rome at the head of his army.

All the time Cleopatra was in Rome, she kept in touch with her ministers. She'd left them in charge of governing Egypt, under the leadership of her vizier. They assured her that all was well at home, so she was content to stay in Rome, waiting for Caesar's return.

It seemed an eternity before he came back, triumphant as always. Cleopatra was overjoyed to see him again and hoped that life would continue as before.

But things had changed.

Some of Rome's important men felt Caesar had got a bit above himself. He was, they said, acting like a king.

'Nonsense,' said Cleopatra. 'You've already told them you won't make yourself King,' she said.

Caesar was not so confident. 'They think I have too much power,' he said.

One dreadful day in March 44 BC, Cleopatra was reading reports from Alexandria. All was peaceful in Egypt and she felt relaxed and happy. Suddenly, there was a commotion outside her door. A woman screamed.

'Charmion, see what's happening!' Cleopatra ordered.

But before the handmaid could move, the door opened and white-faced guards brought in a messenger.

He fell to his knees. 'Highness, I bring terrible news.'

'Speak.' Cleopatra seemed calm, but she had a feeling of dread.

'Great Caesar is dead.'

Her legs trembled. Her heart seemed to somersault. 'Dead? How?'

The sorry story came out. Two Roman senators, Brutus and Cassius, had led a group of men who surrounded Caesar in the Senate, and stabbed him. Again and again they had struck him. The great general had fallen to the floor, his toga drenched in blood.

The next few days were wretched for Cleopatra and her Egyptian entourage. It wasn't safe to be on the streets. Rome seemed full of suspicion and fear.

After Caesar's funeral, which was organised by his great friend, Mark Antony, Cleopatra considered her future. She couldn't stay in Rome without her protector. She must return to Egypt.

'We're going home,' she told Charmion and Eiras. 'Tell the servants to pack, and tell the captain to prepare for sea.'

Three days later, she could stand it no more. The servants seemed to be working so slowly. 'Tell them to hurry, Eiras,' she said. 'The ship is ready, and I'm afraid to stay any longer.'

'Highness, don't worry,' said Eiras. 'Surely there's no rush. Who would harm you – a queen?'

Cleopatra snapped, 'A queen is always in danger. I never forget it, and neither should you. You are too close to me. If I die, it's more than likely that you will die, too. Remember that!'

12
Running from Rome

Cleopatra was exhausted after the long sea voyage home. She'd had so much to think about. Her advisers would have to be told the latest news. They'd hear that Caesar's will had never mentioned Caesarion. That hurt. But she knew they'd be far more interested to learn that Caesar had adopted his great-nephew, Octavian, who was now his heir.

Once they were settled back home in the palace and she'd had a lovely long bath, Cleopatra called her ministers to the throne room.

'Caesar's death,' she explained, 'means I no longer have any protection. I was safe while my enemies had the might of Rome to answer to if they threatened me.'

'Your armies are strong, Highness,' said one. 'You have little to fear.'

Cleopatra stared at him coldly. 'It's not threats from outside that I fear,' she snapped, 'it's threats from inside. Inside this palace. What's to stop my husband killing me, and making himself the only ruler?' Her voice rose. 'He might bring Arsinoë back, and marry her! What then of my son, Caesarion? What will happen to him?'

There was silence.

'Come on,' she said. 'You are my advisers. Advise me!'

The vizier asked to speak with her alone. Cleopatra waved the others away.

'I am thinking,' the vizier said slowly, 'that it's a pity your son, Caesarion, is not king. If he was, his position would be secure. After all, he is the heir to your throne.'

Cleopatra pondered for a moment, then said, 'But that cannot be. My husband is Egypt's king.'

'Only while he lives...'

'I see.' Cleopatra left the room in silence.

Just weeks afterwards, in midsummer 44 BC, the queen was told that her husband, King Ptolemy XIV, had been found dead.

'Poisoned, you think?' she asked the vizier, when he broke the news.

'It is possible, Highness. Who can tell?'

They looked into each other's eyes for a moment. Then Cleopatra said, 'I must have a king to rule beside me. Clearly, I haven't had time to think about this. My husband's death has come as a great shock.'

'Naturally, Highness.'

'So what do you suggest?'

The adviser cleared his throat. 'It might be best to make your son, Caesarion, your co-ruler, Highness.'

Cleopatra smiled. 'What a perfect solution!'

So little Caesarion was created King Ptolemy XV. His mother could now rule exactly as she wished, with her toddler king beside her.

'Caesarion is my link with Rome,' she thought. 'They'll still be our friends. Arsinoë is in exile, and there's no one who's entitled to claim my throne. I'm safe at last.'

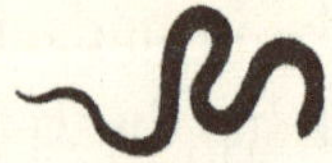

Life was peaceful for the next couple of years. But those years weren't without problems. The Nile didn't flood properly. That meant the land wasn't watered and made fertile, so crops didn't grow and animals died. The people weren't happy. Plague swept through the land, causing illness and death. They raged against Cleopatra.

'She's a goddess, isn't she?' they complained. 'Why doesn't she make the river flood and stop us starving?'

But by this time, Cleopatra had other worries.

'I've had a request from Brutus and Cassius,' she told her council. 'They were responsible for Caesar's death, and now they want soldiers and food from my country.'

'Who are they fighting?' her vizier asked.

'Other Romans! Especially Mark Antony, Caesar's friend. Brutus says Antony has joined with Octavian and they want to take control of Rome. Oh, what should I do?'

To add to her confusion, days later she got a message from Mark Antony. He wanted help, too.

'Give us your support, Queen Cleopatra, and I promise that when we win, we'll protect you, just as great Caesar did.'

'Now what?' Cleopatra complained. 'I *want* to support Antony and Octavian, but suppose they lose? Then Brutus and Cassius and all of Rome will be my enemies.'

But she made her decision. Roman soldiers, left in Egypt by Caesar, were sent to help Mark Antony.

Cleopatra waited anxiously, hoping she'd backed the winner. Then one day not long afterwards, a servant came running to Charmion and Eiras. 'Hurry to your mistress!' he cried.

Charmion went pale. 'Is she hurt?'

'No, she's mad with rage!'

The two handmaids flew to the queen, and did all they could to soothe her fury. 'What's happened, Highness?' said Charmion, patting lavender oil on Cleopatra's forehead, while Eiras poured her a cool drink.

'My army has gone over to Cassius' side,' she spat. 'I hope they all die of snakebites. And now the man has the nerve to ask for *more* men.' She knocked Charmion's hands away. 'Fetch my scribe.'

Cleopatra dictated a letter to Cassius, telling him she was short of manpower herself. 'People are sick. We have plague and famine here. I can't help you any more. You already have most of my army.' Next, she ordered a fleet of warships to be made ready. 'We'll sail to help Antony and Octavian,' she said.

'We?' said Eiras.

'Yes, we. I'm going, too.'

Eventually, the fleet set sail for Greece, where the battle between the two Roman sides raged. But on the way the weather turned sour. Cleopatra became ill, and the final straw was when a horrendous storm blew up.

The ships were tossed and thrown, and many lives were lost – men washed overboard by gigantic waves. Cleopatra stayed in her cabin, feeling sicker and sicker. Everyone was afraid, and called on the gods to calm the sea.

Finally, in response to a plea by the captain of her own ship, the queen gave the order: 'Return to Alexandria.'

As the battered and broken warships reached quieter waters off Egypt's coast, Cleopatra decided that she was *finished* with Antony and Octavian. 'Let them fight their own battle,' she thought, miserably. 'They must lose. I'm done with Rome.'

13
Cleopatra Takes Control

Towards the end of 42 BC, Cleopatra's fleet of new and repaired warships was almost ready when word came that the Roman war was over. It had ended with a great battle at Philippi, in Greece.

Lying back in her bath, Cleopatra laughed in delight. 'Ladies! Antony and Octavian are the victors. The murderers, Brutus and Cassius, are dead. They killed themselves and saved everyone else the trouble!'

'And are Antony and Octavian friends of Egypt or not?' Eiras asked. 'I've lost track.'

Cleopatra sat up. 'They're the most powerful men in the Roman Empire,' she said. 'I need them as friends. Especially Antony. Octavian's in charge of the western Roman empire, and Antony the east.' She stepped out of the bath. 'Octavian can stay in Rome for all I care. Antony must be my friend and Egypt's protector, just as Caesar was.'

Cleopatra was congratulating herself on the way things had worked out, when she received a letter from Mark Antony that knocked the smile from her face.

'He dares – he *dares* – to order me to travel right across the Mediterranean Sea to visit him at Tarsus!' she stormed to her council. 'He *demands* that I explain why I helped Cassius. Demands! Anyway, Cassius helped himself! To *my soldiers*!'

The ministers tried to soothe her. 'He wants to make you feel bad so you'll help him in his next battle,' said one.

'What battle?'

'He's been raising money so he can afford to pay for men, food and weapons, because he plans to invade Parthia, far to the east.'

Cleopatra thought for a moment. 'That could be true. I remember Caesar desperately wanting to conquer the Parthians.' She stepped down from the dais. Her council flung themselves forward and bowed deeply.

'I'll go,' she said. 'I'll offer him help but, take note, there'll be a price to pay.' Then she stalked out.

But as she strode through the great palace halls with her ladies scurrying behind, she was thinking that Antony *was* rather attractive.

Charmion was shocked that her mistress planned to obey the Roman. Cleopatra only smiled. 'I shall not go to him. I'll find a way to make Antony come to me. You'll see.'

After a long sea journey, Cleopatra's barge sailed upriver to Tarsus, where Antony waited. At every farm or village, people ran to the river's edge. They'd never seen anything like it! The huge golden ship with a towering purple sail sped through the water, rowed by silver oars. As the vessel passed, clouds of perfume filled the air and music floated on the breeze.

When the ship docked in the town harbour,

crowds flocked to see it. So this was how the great Egyptian queen travelled!

Cleopatra put her plan into action. When Antony's invitation to dine reached her, she refused. Instead, she asked him to come to her, as her guest.

Before long, the reply came. Antony accepted.

'You see, Charmion?' Cleopatra spun round, her golden cloak swirling behind her. 'I spoke the truth. I didn't obey Antony's order to go to him. I made him come to me!'

That evening, Antony stepped aboard the most amazing ship he'd ever seen. Everywhere he looked, flames of countless torches were reflected in gold. Scent filled the air. He was in no doubt – this was the vessel of a powerful and wealthy queen.

However, when he was shown into Cleopatra's stateroom, he felt as if he was in the presence of someone who was more than a queen. She lounged on silk cushions beneath a canopy that sparkled with gold thread, dressed as the goddess Isis. She looked beautiful.

The pair drank, feasted and talked under the stars until late. Before they parted, each knew that they would meet again. Cleopatra wanted Antony as her ally. Antony wanted Cleopatra's help in his forthcoming battle. Neither realised just how much they were going to mean to each other.

During the following days, Antony and Cleopatra became very close. Finally, they struck a deal.

'I'll support you, Antony,' she promised, 'in your war against Parthia. You'll have the help you need from Egypt.'

He kissed the inside of her wrist. 'My love, thank you.'

'But I want something in return.'

He knelt and held his arms wide. 'Anything!'

Cleopatra smiled. 'I ask you to do the same for me as Caesar did. I want you, and Rome, to protect me. I need to know I'm safe on my throne, and that you'll help if ever my land is attacked.'

'You have my word. But with your son ruling beside you, who can take your throne? Who has a claim to it?'

Cleopatra looked straight at him. 'Arsinoë.'

'Your sister? But she's in –'

'Exile. I know.' She stroked Antony's hand. 'But while Arsinoë lives, others may like to see her queen instead of me. Dearest, she threatens my life.'

Slowly, Antony nodded. 'I understand. But –'

Cleopatra pouted. 'You did promise me anything…'

14
Antony and Cleopatra

No one spoke of Arsinoë until, one day in 41 BC, Antony came to the queen and said, 'Your sister won't trouble you again.'

Cleopatra pressed her lips together and said nothing. She didn't want to hear any more. All she knew was that Arsinoë was certainly dead.

'But it wasn't on my orders,' she consoled herself in bed that night. 'I didn't ask Antony to have her killed. It was his idea.' She turned over and slept peacefully.

Soon after, Cleopatra returned to Egypt. To her delight, Antony followed a few weeks later. Her new lover quickly settled into Alexandria, enjoying the luxurious palace life. He decided to spend the winter there, instead of returning to his wife, Fulvia, in Rome.

And so began the happiest of times for the young queen. Antony and Cleopatra were in love. They spent long evenings together, eating, chatting and playing games. Sometimes they were alone, but they also enjoyed the company of friends, when they would feast with entertainment from acrobats and dancing girls. After a late night, they'd laze in bed in the mornings, but often they'd get up early and go hunting.

Antony loved wandering round the city, which was something Cleopatra had never done.

'We'll go out in disguise!' he suggested. And this became one of their favourite pastimes. It was such fun!

With Antony, Cleopatra could almost forget being royal. But in spring, their carefree life came to an end when Antony decided to return to Rome. There were problems between the leaders over the division of conquered countries. Antony didn't want anyone taking his lands away from him. They were his source of wealth and power.

Cleopatra wanted him to stay, of course. But, as

queen, she understood how affairs of state almost always came first. And, anyway, she had something wonderful to look forward to. She was expecting twins!

The following year, Cleopatra gave birth to a boy and a girl, both healthy. 'I'll call my son Alexander, after my great ancestor,' she said cradling the babies in her arms.

'Perfect!' said Eiras.

'My daughter will be named Cleopatra, of course.'

Nurses were found for little Alexander and Cleopatra. Their mother and older brother played with them often. But all the time, Cleopatra waited for Antony to come.

'I believed he loved me,' she moaned to her ladies as she stood on the windy harbour wall, hoping for the sight of her lover's ship out at sea.

'He does love you, Highness,' they'd reply. 'How can he not love you?'

The vizier quaked in his sandals.

'Speak, man,' said Cleopatra. 'What's so dreadful

that you're afraid to tell me?'

He took a deep breath. 'Highness, this very day, Mark Antony is getting married.'

The queen laughed. 'Fool! He is already married, to Fulvia.'

The man was silent.

Cleopatra's heart leapt. 'Speak!'

'The lady Fulvia joined forces with Antony's brother. They tried to take power from Octavian.'

'And failed?'

'Yes. Failed. Fulvia fled to Athens and met Antony there. But she became ill, and died.'

Now Cleopatra drew a deep breath. 'So Antony was free?'

'Free, yes, but after Fulvia's treachery, he had to prove his loyalty to Octavian. Highness, I'm afraid to tell you, but I must. He's marrying Octavian's sister.'

Cleopatra collapsed back into her seat. 'Antony was free to marry, and he chose *Octavia*?'

Then she screamed.

The servants had never known the queen in such a weeping rage. The only time she was calm was when she sent for her babies.

'Little ones,' she told the twins, 'your father has deserted us. But nothing can change the fact that you're half Roman.' She waved her women away. 'Together,' she whispered to the babies, 'we'll rule our own Egyptian-Roman empire. You'll see.'

Three years passed. Cleopatra devoted herself to Egypt, its people and her children. She held meetings, made decisions, gave orders and signed documents with the phrase she always used: 'Let it be so'. Peaceful Egypt became richer and richer under her reign. Even when the harvest was bad, there was enough gold to trade with other countries for food.

Meanwhile, Antony was learning that Octavian couldn't always be relied upon. They'd agreed that Antony would give Octavian warships in exchange for 20,000 soldiers to fight against the Parthians, who he was yet to conquer.

But although Antony kept his side of the bargain, Octavian never sent the promised men. So there was Antony, short of a hundred warships, and short of soldiers, too.

He turned to the one person he felt would help him – Cleopatra.

The queen had mixed feelings when Antony asked her to join him in Syria. Did he still love her? Did he just need her help? Perhaps it was both. But she longed to see him.

She sailed for Antioch at the far eastern end of the Mediterranean sea and the first thing she did was to tell her advisers, 'Find out where Antony's wife is. I don't wish to see her.'

The reply pleased her. 'Highness, Octavia has been sent back to Rome, where her brother will look after her until Antony's return. It's for her health.'

Cleopatra spoke sharply. 'She's sick?'

The adviser cleared his throat. 'Er, not exactly, Highness.'

'What then? Oh, don't tell me, let me guess – she's expecting a child.'

The adviser bowed.

'No matter.' Cleopatra smiled. With Octavia out of the way, she'd have Antony all to herself. But first she must find out what he wanted. As if she didn't know.

15
Magnificent Gifts

'You say you love me, Antony, but there's something more. Tell the truth. I'll know if you don't.'

'Cleopatra, I do love you, but I cannot lie. I need help.'

'The usual,' said the queen. 'Am I right? Soldiers, food, weapons, warships?'

'Yes.'

'You may have them,' said Cleopatra, 'but, once more, I want something in return.'

Antony hugged her. 'Anything, my love!'

Cleopatra smiled. 'Lands that once belonged to my Ptolemy ancestors are in Roman hands. I want them back.'

'Lands?'

'Cyprus. Crete. Cilicia. Shall I go on?' said Cleopatra. 'No. My scribe can list them.'

She clapped her hands, and an elderly man entered carrying writing materials. Cleopatra dictated, and Antony watched in silence as the list grew. When it was done, he looked at Cleopatra, aghast. 'All that?'

She smiled. 'I'll leave you to think about it … my love.'

Antony was so desperate for support in his forthcoming battle that Cleopatra knew she'd get her way. She danced across the room, waving the signed papyrus that gave her almost everything she'd demanded.

'Fetch one of my jewel boxes!' she commanded Eiras.

The handmaid knelt with an open sandalwood box held to her forehead.

Cleopatra chose some rings, earrings and bracelets, and scattered them on a nearby table.

'Charmion, Eiras, choose something for yourselves!'

The ladies gasped. 'Highness!'

'Today I am queen of many new lands. That makes me rich beyond the dreams of … oh, any of you mortals!'

She immediately ordered that Antony should have the men and supplies he needed. The lovers took up their relationship where they'd left off, and in the weeks that followed they were hardly ever apart.

Antony adored his children. The twins were now three years old, and it took them a while to get used to calling this strange man 'Daddy'.

'They're beautiful, Cleopatra,' Antony said. 'Let's have a special ceremony to show the people that I'm their father. We'll give them special names!'

'What do you suggest?' asked Cleopatra.

Antony thought. 'Alexander shall be named after the sun. He will be Alexander Helios.'

Cleopatra clapped her hands, delighted. 'I love it. And we'll name our daughter after the moon. She shall be Cleopatra Selene!'

Though the lovers were together again, it couldn't last. Antony had to fight the Parthians, and Cleopatra had to go home.

However, it wasn't long before she realised she was expecting another baby, due that summer. 'I'm so happy,' she told young Caesarion. 'I have you, the heir to my kingdom. I have my beautiful twins, and Antony loves me. Everything is wonderful.'

When her baby was born, in 36 BC, she named him Ptolemy Philadelphos. All she needed for complete happiness was for Antony to defeat the Parthians quickly and return to Alexandria.

Then, one day, not long afterwards, when sand was blowing in from the desert, whistling through windows and blasting walls, a message came.

Antony had lost his battle and was on his way to Egypt. It was a disaster. Almost half his men were either dead or had been taken prisoner. When Antony reached Alexandria, there was nothing Cleopatra could do or say that would cheer him. He was exhausted and mentally drained.

'You'll fight again,' she said. 'You'll win!'

'But what sort of a leader am I now?' he moaned. 'My men have no faith in me. Would you follow a general who's likely to lead you to your death?'

Cleopatra did her best to make Antony believe in himself again, and in time he decided that he would tackle the Parthians once more. If only Octavian would send the troops he'd promised, he could get going.

'I've won battles before. I'll win them again!' he said.

Cleopatra kissed him. 'That's my Antony!'

Eventually the news he had been waiting for arrived. Octavia was on her way with troops and ships from Octavian, as promised, along with her own money, and food she'd paid for herself.

But Antony was livid. 'She's only bringing 2,000 men. Octavian promised me *20,000*!'

Cleopatra went pale. Antony could never attack the Parthians with so few men. 'What will you do?'

'Scribe!' he yelled. 'What will I do? I'll send her back to Rome or Athens or wherever, and she can send the men on to me.'

He was in such a fury that Cleopatra decided it wasn't the right time to offer advice. She was glad Octavia had been sent packing. But she knew Octavian would be livid. His sister, publicly rejected by her husband! How humiliating!

When Cleopatra did get round to telling Antony what she thought of his actions, he replied, 'I don't care what Octavian thinks. He's let me down. I only married Octavia to please her brother.'

Cleopatra's heart leapt. 'Darling, is that true?'

'Of course,' he growled. 'You know I love only you.'

Antony wasn't equipped to attack the Parthians, but he managed to score a smaller victory in Armenia. When he returned with the Armenian royal family as prisoners, together with cartloads of treasure, he felt enormously bucked up.

'Your father's coming home a hero,' Cleopatra told the children. 'We'll be there to greet him, and I'll wear my crown –'

'And three cobras on your head!' said Caesarion.

Cleopatra laughed. 'Yes, I'll wear my uraeus, and sit on a golden throne, set on a silver platform. The people will see how much I honour him.'

The people also saw how much Antony honoured their queen. A grand ceremony was held, where Antony declared that Caesarion was Julius Caesar's true son and heir. 'He should be in Octavian's place!' he declared.

As if that wasn't enough to anger the Romans, Antony's children were given their own lands.

Cleopatra Selene's lands included the island of Crete, and Ptolemy Philadelphos was presented with, among other territories, Syria and Cilicia. Alexander Helios received several lands, including the newly conquered Armenia, and also found himself ruler of Parthia, even though it hadn't yet been added to the Roman lands.

That night, Antony and Cleopatra held a banquet to celebrate their greatness.

'One thing's for sure,' Cleopatra thought, as Eiras got her ready for bed. 'Octavian won't like it.'

16
Battle at Actium

'He *what*?' Antony was shaking with fury.

The kneeling messenger trembled.

Cleopatra touched Antony's arm. 'Getting angry won't help,' she said. 'Sit down and talk to me. You can't blame Octavian for saying bad things about you. He's got it into his head that we want to rule over everyone.'

'Exactly! Messenger, tell the queen what else he said.'

The man swallowed. 'He said something like, "What's she going to do next? Make herself Cleopatra, Queen of Rome?"' He ducked swiftly as Antony's sandalled foot swung towards his ear.

Cleopatra dismissed the messenger. 'You can

understand the Romans being angry. After all, you gave some of their lands away. It's bound to cause trouble.'

Antony paced up and down. 'But Octavian's seen my will! No one should be allowed to do that. I left it in the care of the vestal virgins. Anything they look after is sacred!'

Cleopatra's eyes were cold. 'Money opens many doors, my love. Anyway, why does it matter if he saw your will?'

Antony sat against a cool marble pillar and put his head in his hands. 'I left property – lands – to our children. But in Roman eyes, they're foreigners.'

Cleopatra nodded. 'Then I can see why he's angry. What else?'

'I … I said when … when I…'

'What? Don't mumble.'

Antony took a deep breath. 'I said when I die, I want to be buried here in Egypt.'

Cleopatra gasped. 'You're cutting yourself off from Rome! The people must be feeling so betrayed.' She held her arms out. 'But it's very sweet that you want to end your days with me.'

'Oh, my love, I do.'

They kissed, then Cleopatra walked to the door. As the guards opened it, she turned and said, 'Of course, you do realise this will mean war!'

In the days and weeks that followed, Antony and Cleopatra made preparations. Octavian would declare war on Antony, they knew. And they would be ready.

A large battle fleet had to be prepared. Antony and Cleopatra travelled to Ephesus, to the east of Greece. There their ships would gather, ready if Octavian made a move. Antony also assembled his army. With Roman soldiers and Egypt's famed warships, they could vanquish anyone!

'We'll base ourselves in Greece,' said Cleopatra. 'We'll attack when Octavian's fleet sets sail for Egypt.'

But first they stopped off on Samos, a beautiful Greek island, where they organised a huge festival of music, theatre, singing and dancing. They wanted Octavian to hear about it, and see how happy and confident and unafraid they were.

The fleet sailed to different harbours along the

western coast of Greece, just across the sea from Italy. Then Cleopatra and Antony waited in Athens, near the home of the queen's ancestors.

One day, later in 32 BC, Antony burst in on Cleopatra. When she saw his face, she dismissed her ladies at once.

'What is it?' she asked.

'Octavian has declared war.'

Cleopatra turned towards the sea. 'So, it's beginning. But why are you so agitated, Antony? We knew this would happen – you've even divorced Octavia. We're well prepared.'

Antony looked Cleopatra straight in the eyes. 'He's declared war, but not on me. On you!'

Cleopatra nearly exploded. 'After all I've done for those Romans! I supported Pompey, and Octavian – curse him! I did whatever Caesar wanted. I bore his child, for goodness' sake! Haven't I helped out every time *you* needed me? And now this … this puny upstart declares war on *me*?'

She took a wine goblet and flung it at the wall. 'Come, Antony. We'll give him war.'

Cleopatra may have despised Octavian, but she learned to respect the man who directed the Roman fleet. His name was Agrippa, and he was an experienced and intelligent man.

Before long, he'd attacked and taken several of the ports where the Egyptian warships were based. Then Octavian's soldiers landed on the Greek mainland.

Antony and Cleopatra hurried north with their forces to Actium, on a small peninsula. Octavian responded by marching his men south, to face the enemy across a narrow stretch of water that was the entrance to the Gulf of Ambracia.

Actium was a bad place. It was swampy and mosquito-ridden, and soon men began to fall ill, even die. Worse, Cleopatra's supply ships were being attacked from land and sea.

This was disastrous. Without food and other essentials, the Egyptian forces began to weaken, and the men started to desert their leaders.

Antony brought his fleet through the narrow stretch of water into the safety of the Gulf, while both sides prepared for a land battle.

But Agrippa pounced. He sailed some of his

ships to block the entrance to the Gulf, and there he stayed – for weeks. More and more of the Egyptian army deserted, and hunger became a serious problem; it was impossible for Cleopatra's supply ships to get past Agrippa and food was running out.

One of Antony's generals said they should leave the fleet and march north – get away and live to fight another day.

'I won't leave my fleet to those Romans,' Cleopatra said. 'We'll return to Egypt and make plans for another battle.' She ordered all her treasure to be loaded onto her own ship.

Between them, Antony, Cleopatra and the senior officers came up with a plan. Antony would sail his ships out of the Gulf into open sea, straight towards Agrippa's fleet, as if they were going to fight. When they'd drawn them away from the entrance to the Gulf, Cleopatra would take her ships and make a run for it.

But Agrippa was ready. He spread his fleet out so it was almost impossible for Cleopatra to get through and, of course, he attacked. But as battle began, the queen saw her chance.

'Captain, head for that gap in the Roman line,' she cried. 'Tell your oarsmen to row for their lives!'

With two of Agrippa's ships bearing down on them, Cleopatra's fast treasure ship burst through the gap and into open sea. Her fleet burst through behind her, but most of the ships Antony was commanding were trapped by Agrippa's line. As her crew raised the sails, Cleopatra looked back at the battle scene, shading her eyes. Where *was* Antony?

Her heart leapt as another vessel surged through the Roman fleet. It wasn't Antony's ship, but there was a familiar figure on board. 'Antony?' she cried. 'It's Antony!'

Her joy gave way to misgivings. Antony had escaped by transferring to a smaller ship, yes, but in doing so he'd deserted his men and left them to perish or be taken prisoner. How would he live with such shame?

17
Desperate Days

Antony was in despair, and nothing Cleopatra could do or say could help. News arrived that many of his surviving soldiers had changed sides and were now fighting for Octavian. Most of the Egyptian ships were burnt, destroyed or sunk. He locked himself away with his shame and misery and spent days and nights in a lonely house on the edge of the sea. Not even the queen could persuade him out.

Cleopatra wasn't one to sit around sulking. She was duty-bound to protect her country. She still had her treasure, so she ordered shipbuilders to repair what ships they could, and to build fast new ones as quickly as possible.

Like all Egyptian pharaohs, Cleopatra had a

magnificent mausoleum, where her body would be placed when she died. This tomb was a good safe place to keep the rest of her treasure.

When she heard that Octavian was in Phoenicia, on the eastern coastline of the Mediterranean, she instantly guessed why.

She sent for Antony. 'Please come back to the palace,' went the message. 'I need your advice.'

Eventually, Antony returned.

'Octavian's marching to attack Egypt,' she told him. 'What am I to do? You have barely any men, and my fleet isn't ready. How will I fight Octavian?'

'You won't,' said Antony.

Cleopatra gasped. 'You've given up. Haven't you? *Haven't you*?'

Antony didn't reply.

Cleopatra took him to a quiet room, where they talked for hours. Finally, they decided that the only way to handle the situation was to make a deal with Octavian.

'I'll promise to give up my throne if he'll spare my life and let Caesarion rule instead of me,' she said. 'He'll surely agree. After all, Caesarion *is* half Roman.'

Cleopatra sent her messengers and waited … and waited. Octavian didn't even bother to reply.

Then Antony sent rich gifts, offering to give up soldiering and live in Greece. Still there was no reply.

The two lovers were completely unsettled by Octavian's silence, and didn't know what to do next. Cleopatra sent a string of hugely expensive gifts, and even offered a huge chunk of her treasure. Octavian continued to ignore her.

When the news came that the Roman army was almost at Alexandria's gates, Antony gathered all his strength and courage and rode out, with what soldiers he had left, to defend the city.

Cleopatra was distraught. She knew it would end in tragedy. 'My Antony's gone,' she wailed. 'Charmion! Eiras! And you,' she cried, pointing at a serving man. 'Hurry. We're going to my mausoleum.'

The servants didn't believe they'd be safe inside the mausoleum, but they had to obey.

The building had no windows on the ground floor and, once the entrance was barricaded, the queen and her servants fled upstairs, where they could look out from a high window.

Now came ghastly news, shouted up by one

of Antony's serving men. 'Highness, when Lord Antony heard you were in your tomb, he thought you were dead.'

'Oh, tell him I'm alive,' she cried, 'and tell him to come here. We'll be safe and we'll be together.'

The man shook his head. 'Highness, Lord Antony was so distressed, he told his servant, Eros, to kill him with his own sword.'

Cleopatra gasped. 'No! He didn't!'

'He didn't, Highness. Eros killed himself instead, but Antony wouldn't be put off. He held a sword to his body, and fell onto it. He's badly wounded. Really badly.'

As Cleopatra wept, Eiras called down, 'You! Bring Antony here, dead or alive!'

Half an hour later, Antony had been hauled up to the window by the queen's serving man and ladies, and now lay bleeding in Cleopatra's arms. Moments later, he died.

Shortly afterwards, one of Octavian's most trusted men, Proculeius, arrived at the mausoleum.

'Ask your mistress to come down to the door!' he called. 'She needn't open it, but I'd like to speak with her.'

Cleopatra, desperate to find a way out of this mess, ran downstairs. 'What do you wish to say to me?' she demanded, her head held high.

Proculeius spoke through the door, explaining that he'd been sent by Octavian. 'My master wishes you to leave this place, and return to your palace.'

'So he can kill me and take my treasure?' she shouted. 'Never! I am the queen! I will not give myself up!' She paused, then said, 'Wait.' She leaned her forehead against the cool wall, thinking.

Charmion went to her. 'Highness?'

Cleopatra brushed her aside and went to the door. 'Are you still there?'

'I am,' replied Proculeius.

'Do one thing for me,' Cleopatra said in a quieter voice. 'Please, ask Octavian to spare my children. Let my son inherit my kingdom.'

'I will do as you ask,' said Proculeius, and he left.

The next day, another man, Gallus, came to talk to her. He, too, tried to persuade Cleopatra to give herself up. Whenever she asked what Octavian's response was to her plea, he skirted round the subject. He talked on and on.

Suddenly, Charmion screamed, 'They're coming to get you!'

Cleopatra turned to see that Proculeius and two other men had managed to get into the mausoleum. They'd put a ladder up to the window and climbed in while everyone was downstairs.

Cleopatra refused to be taken prisoner. She grabbed the little dagger she'd started wearing in her belt, and tried to stab herself. But Proculeius stopped her. He even frisked her clothing, to see if she'd hidden anything there, like poison. Octavian wanted her alive.

The queen was moved, under guard, to the palace, and only allowed out for Antony's funeral. Shortly afterwards, she became ill and stopped eating. Nothing any of her servants did or said could persuade her otherwise.

When she heard that she and her children were to be taken to Rome, she became angry and afraid. 'I am a queen! I will *not* be paraded as a prisoner in front of common Romans. It shall not happen.'

She made her plans.

Knowing that this would probably be her last chance, Cleopatra asked permission to visit

Antony's tomb again. She was allowed to do so, under guard, and was then taken back to her rooms at the palace. Afterwards, she spoke to some of her servants, giving particular orders. Everything had to be right.

Her women bathed her, dressed her hair and applied her makeup. Then, dressed in her most regal clothes, Cleopatra ate a good meal. She was just finishing when a man was admitted. He was carrying a gift for the queen.

'I'm just a farmer,' he told the guards. 'All I've got to give Her Highness is this basket of figs.'

A guard lifted the damp leaves that covered the fruit, to check the man was telling the truth. 'They look good!' he said.

Next, Cleopatra produced a letter she'd written to Octavian, and sent it with a messenger. 'Do not hurry,' she said. And she sent away all her servants except Charmion and Eiras, and told the guards to stay outside.

Cleopatra took the basket of figs to a couch, and lay down. 'Charmion, Eiras, my letter asks one thing of Octavian. I want to be buried with Antony,' she said. 'And now the time has come. I will not be shamed and humiliated in Rome. I will end my days in Egypt.'

Eiras let out a sob. She knew that Cleopatra intended to die. 'We won't leave you, Highness,' she said. 'You won't die alone.'

Cleopatra smiled. 'It's all as I planned. Come, ladies, let's examine these beautiful figs.'

She thrust her hand deep among the figs and, almost at once, gasped in pain. Then, from the basket, she drew a snake, and held it out in front of her. Charmion, weeping quietly, took the snake from her hands...

When Octavian's men burst in, they found Charmion, almost too weak to move, trying to set the queen's diadem straight and to tidy stray wisps of her dark hair. Eiras lay at the foot of her mistress' couch, dying.

Cleopatra, herself, lay on her silken couch – dead.

Afterword

Octavian did allow Cleopatra to be buried beside her beloved Antony. Her eldest son, Caesarion, was captured and executed. The twins and little Ptolemy Philadelphos suffered the humiliation their mother couldn't face. They walked, in chains, in Octavian's public triumphal procession. But afterwards Antony's ex-wife, Octavia, took them into her home and raised them with her own children. Cleopatra Selene married well and became a queen in Africa. It's possible that her twin, Alexander, and little Ptolemy went to live with her, but it's also possible that they died young.

Octavian became the Emperor of the whole Roman Empire. He took the name Augustus Caesar, and became a great ruler. And Egypt, with all her wealth, became another province of Rome.

Map

GREECE
Macedonia
ITALY
Philippi
Rome
TURKEY
Actium
Ephesus
Tarsus
Gulf of Ambracia
Samos
Antioch
Athens
CYPRUS
SYRIA
CRETE
Mediterranean Sea
Pharos Island and Lighthouse
Alexandria
Pelusium
CLEOPATRA'S WORLD
River Nile
EGYPT

Index

LIVES in ACTION

LIVES in ACTION

MARTIN HOWARD

Alexander the Great

The story of the mighty Greek conqueror